Fundamentals of Paper Cup Construction

Parker Ruth

This publication is dedicated to
the Davidson Family and Friends
for their support and inspiration.

Contents

Introduction

Welcome to the magnificent world of paper cup construction! In this book, we will explore some of the fundamentals of the amazing art and science of building structures with paper cups. Whether you are a parent looking for an affordable, stimulating toy, a teacher looking for a classroom activity, a manager looking for a team building exercise, or anyone with a sense of curiosity and a playful attitude, this book is perfect for you. But remember: the best way to learn any form of art is simply to give it a try! There's no substitute for hands-on knowledge.

In this introduction, we will explore some of the many wonderful qualities of paper cups as a building medium, as well as some general things to keep in mind for novice cup constructors. In the rest of the book, we will explore the fundamental techniques that can be combined, adapted, and iterated to create amazing structures out of paper cups. Once you have explored the techniques provided here, you will be able to develop your own unique building style. This book only provides a brief introduction to the most rudimentary concepts in the field of paper cup construction; don't be tempted to stop building after you have turned the last page! There will always be more fascinating areas to explore when it comes to paper cups. Now get some cups and start building! The magnificent world of paper cup construction awaits!

Research in developmental psychology has shed light on the types of toys that are most stimulating — that is, those that foster creativity, problem solving, social skills, spatial reasoning, motor skills, etc. It has been found that the best toys are not the ones with big brand labels, lots of accessories, or battery packs. Rather, the best toys for both boys and girls are the simple, constructive toys, like wooden blocks. Not only do construction sets like these incite spatial and mathematical thinking, but their open-ended use makes them perfect for creative expression as well. Thus, building with blocks or other constructive toys is an ideal experience for stimulating young minds.

Sadly, however, building blocks suffer many shortcomings. There are never enough of them to make anything satisfactorily large. And even if there are enough, they take up too much space to store. In addition, they have hard edges and corners that can hurt if stepped on or thrown.

It turns out though, that paper cups have all of the benefits of building blocks, and yet they overcome the aforementioned downfalls as well. Since paper cups are very affordable, it's easy to amass a large collection of them. Furthermore, they can be stored with unparalleled efficiency, since they stack within each other. Finally, paper cups are the most harmless building material imaginable. They are lightweight, round, and smooth. In fact, the top edges are folded over, which prevents paper cuts. One might think that paper cups are less durable than blocks, since they are, after all, made of paper. But paper cups prove to be amazingly durable. If one is crushed, it can easily be popped back into shape no worse for the wear. Cups, therefore, are not only stimulating, affordable, and safe, but they are also reusable, lasting for many years.

Already, it should be clear that paper cups are the ideal medium for developing creativity, cooperation, and critical thinking, but there is one more positive facet of paper cups that merits mention. It is simply that they are simple. Both research and common sense inform us that the best toys are without gimmicky distractions courtesy of the marketing department. When all distractions are removed, the builder is left to focus on what is most important: building. Paper cups are the epitome of simplicity. In all of their extraordinary simplicity, paper cups represent the ideal toy.

Above all else, building with paper cups is really fun. For those skeptics out there, this fact has been proven experimentally; when paper cups are introduced to a crowd, the inevitable result is mirth and joy from youth and adults alike. There is something irresistible about using such a simple and everyday object to create magnificent structures. In fact, knocking them down after they are built is at least half the fun!

Naturally, the first step is to find yourself some paper cups to build with. The standard paper cups for building are the three-ounce variety often found at water coolers. Larger cups can be used to build larger towers more quickly, but they are often undesirable in the long run both because of their size, and their structure. Pleated and conical varieties are very poor for building and should be avoided completely. A remarkable quality of the standard three-ounce paper cup is that it can be crushed and reformed with little damage to its structural integrity. Of course, unnecessarily crushing cups isn't a very good idea, since it raises the risk of tearing them. Though very ambitious towers can require as many as two thousand cups, you will be surprised what you can create with a few dozen at first.

When you're ready to start building, the first thing to do is decide where you will build. Naturally you should work someplace flat. A table may be a good place to start, but the size limitations get in the way quickly. For this reason, building on the ground is usually best. If you do so, however, make sure to choose a floor that will be both relatively smooth, to provide a stable base for your constructions, and also comfortable because you may be kneeling for a good amount of the time. Also, try not to build near doors or places of heavy foot traffic, which can generate inconvenient breezes, unless you are prepared to watch your tower topple. Of course, even after taking all precautions, occasional accidents are to be expected; it's all part of the joy and challenge of paper cup construction. Once you have a collection of cups and a place to work, you can begin building!

Techniques

As you try the techniques described in this section, be careful not to stack multiple cups in the place of one, like in the tower on the left (see if you can find the extra cup). This is wasteful and also can make your towers crooked. To prevent this from happening, try carrying the stack in your left hand while pulling one cup at a time off of the top of the stack with your right hand (or vice-versa for lefties). If you hold your thumb on the rims of the top few cups and give each one a slight twist as you lift it, you will be able to feel if you have separated it from the ones below, optimizing efficiency.

13

Walls

The most basic cup tower is called a wall. On this page you can see some examples of walls. The bottom level of cups is called the base. Notice that the number of cups in a tower's base is also the number of cups it has in height. Unfortunately, large walls have a tendency to fall over, since they act like sails when they catch breezes.

Naturally, you don't have to make walls triangular. Any structure built in a linear way (constructed on top of a line of cups) counts as a wall.

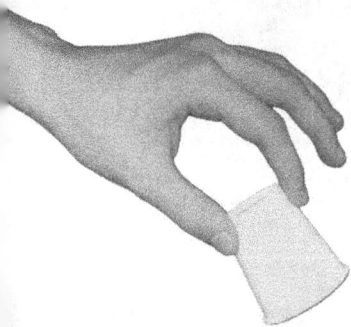

Although walls alone are not the most stable or the most interesting structures that can be built with paper cups, there is a lot that we can learn from them. First, you will notice that each cup in a wall has two other cups underneath (unless it's on the bottom row). This means that each row can only have up to one cup less than the row under it. Thus, a wall can only converge with increasing height. In other words, the tower will only become narrower, as you build higher; it will never become wider.

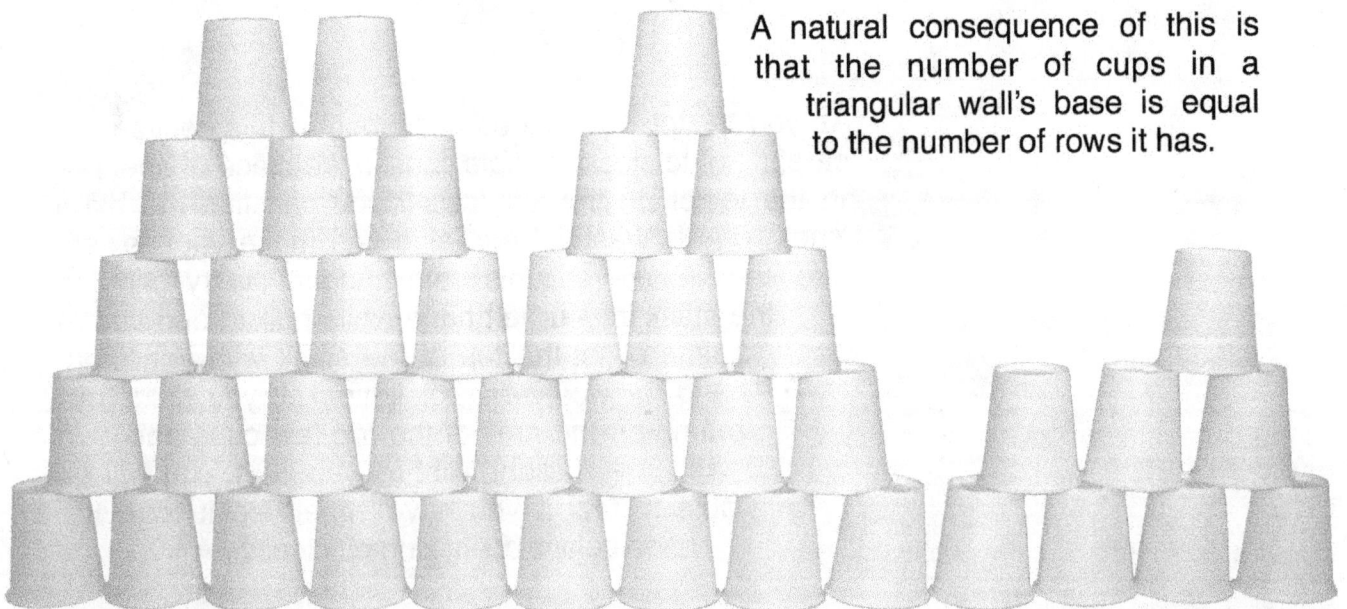

A natural consequence of this is that the number of cups in a triangular wall's base is equal to the number of rows it has.

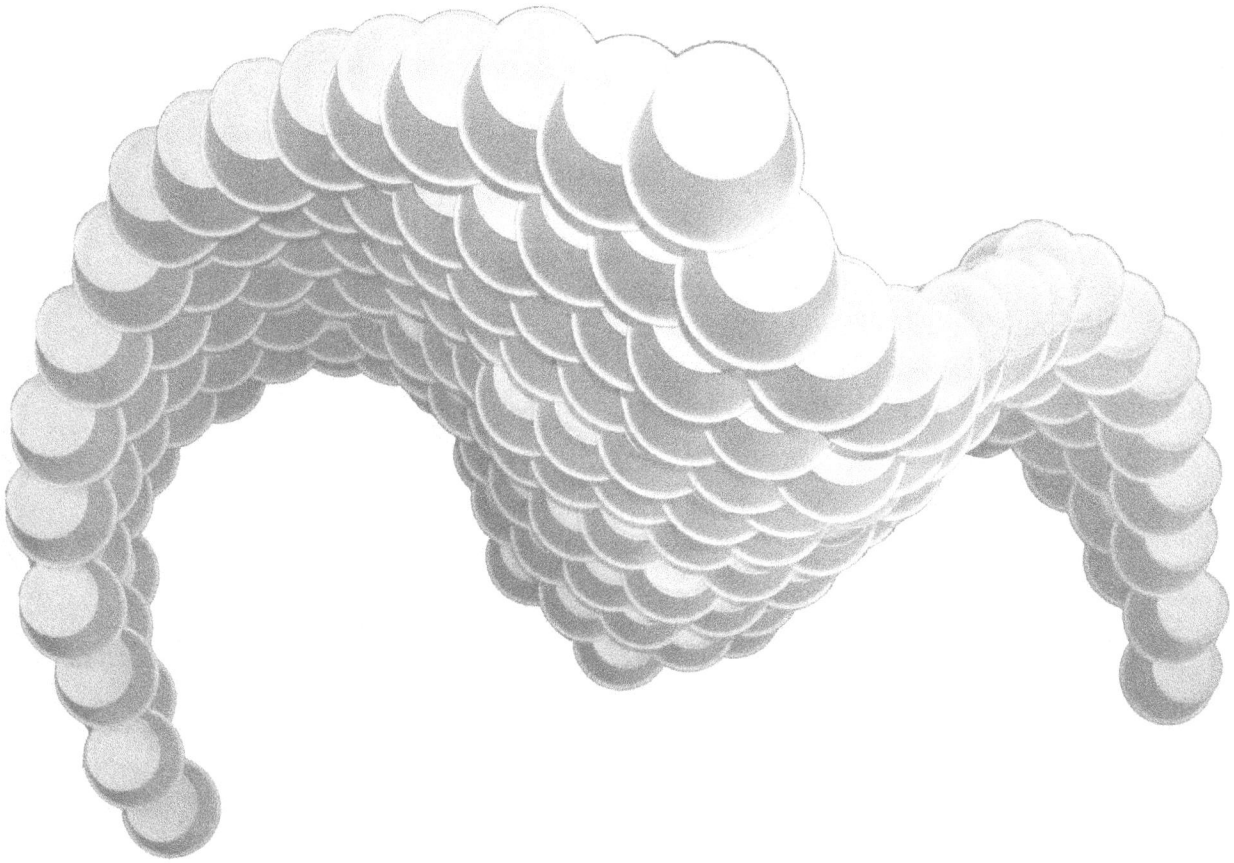

Walls can also be curved like the one you see above. If a wall is curved very tightly, it may develop a tendency to lean outwards. To reduce the likelihood of this happening, space the paper cups apart from each other by about a quarter of an inch.

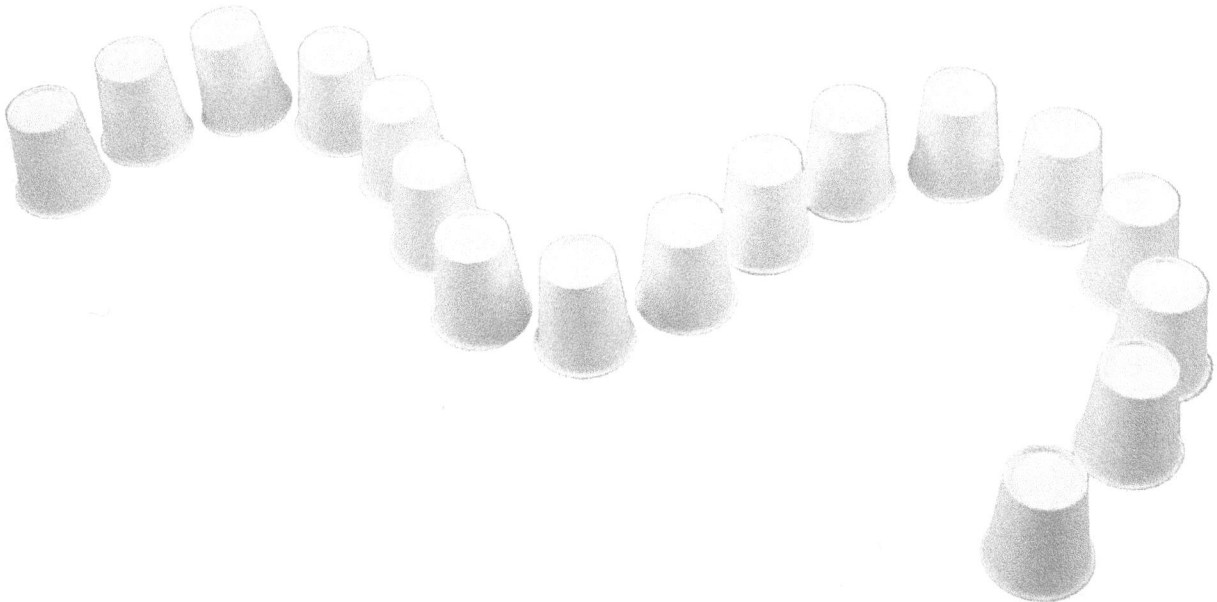

Circles

If you curve a wall around into a circle, it takes on a completely new geometry. No longer does it become narrower the higher it goes. A circle can be built as tall as you like because it remains the same width on each level. Circles are quite practical for building tall constructions because they are very stable – much more so than simple walls.

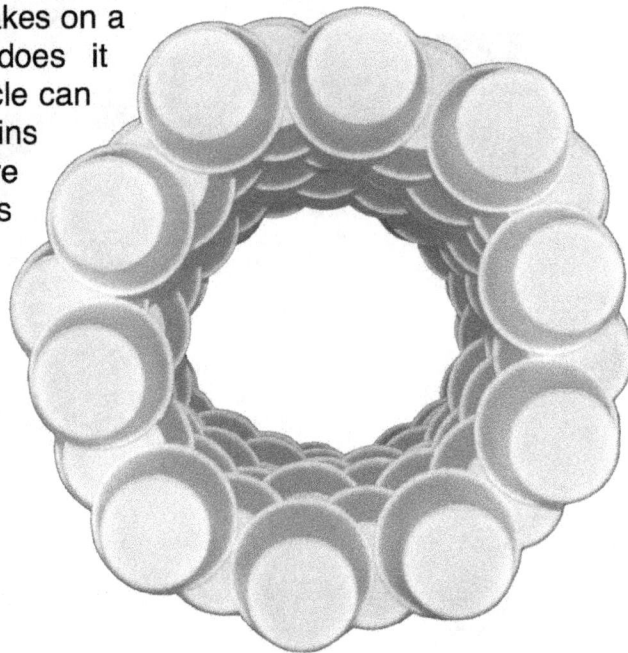

Since circles can theoretically continue growing to an infinite height, you have to decide where and how you want to stop. At bottom of this page you can see a "flat" termination (left), where the tower ends evenly, and a "penne" termination (right), which is named after the type of pasta that has the same shape.

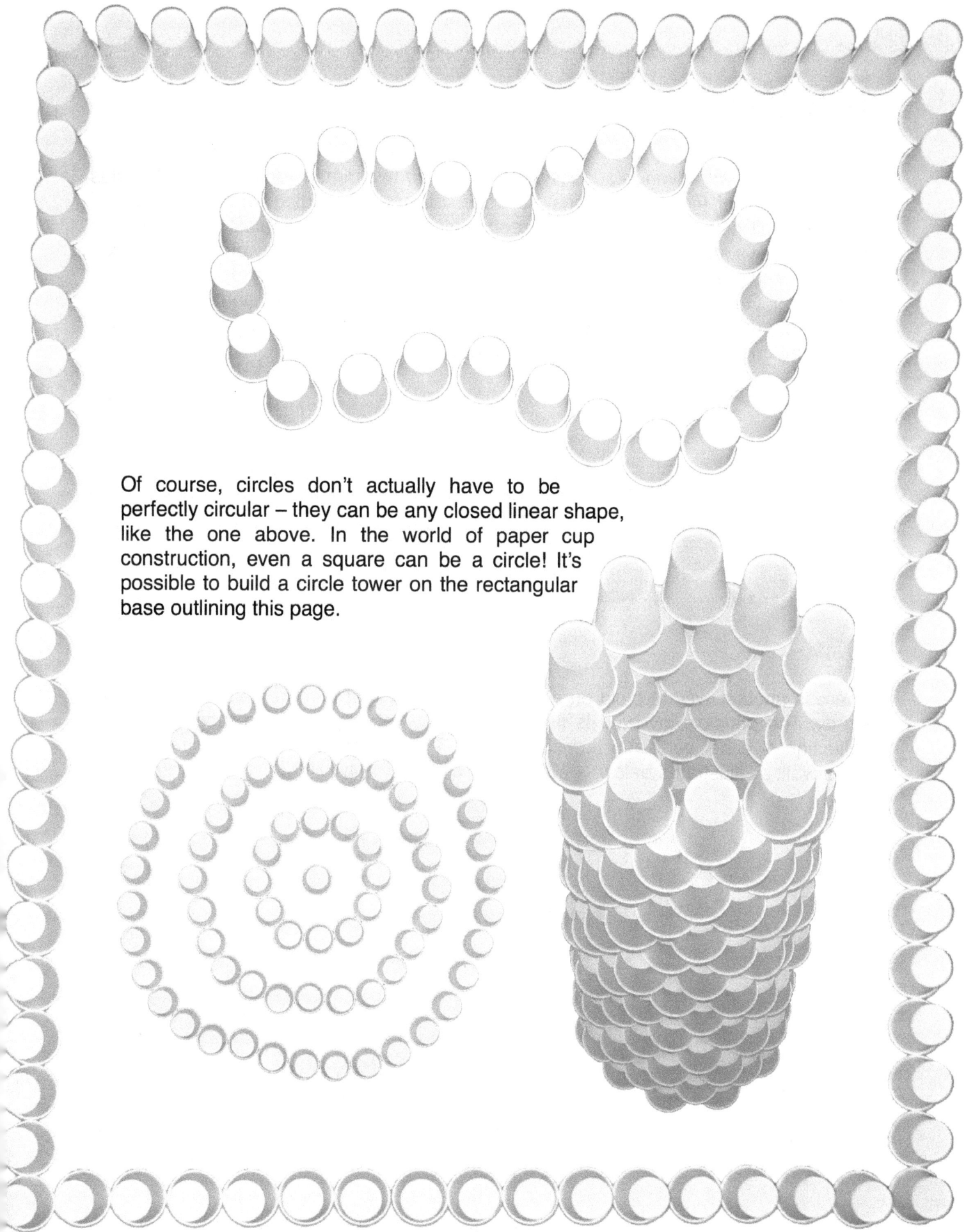

Of course, circles don't actually have to be perfectly circular – they can be any closed linear shape, like the one above. In the world of paper cup construction, even a square can be a circle! It's possible to build a circle tower on the rectangular base outlining this page.

Rectangles

In this section, we advance audaciously from mere two-dimensional walls and circles into the realm of three-dimensional volumes. Instead of building on top of a line of cups, we will now build on top of a rectangular lattice. The simplest rectangle is a square, so let's start with that. One way to build a square tower is by putting every cup on top of four below it. The result is a symmetric four-sided pyramid, much like the pyramids of Giza (we'll talk about three-sided pyramids in a later section). This method is less generally compatible than some other techniques, however, and it can also be somewhat unstable, depending on cup proportions.

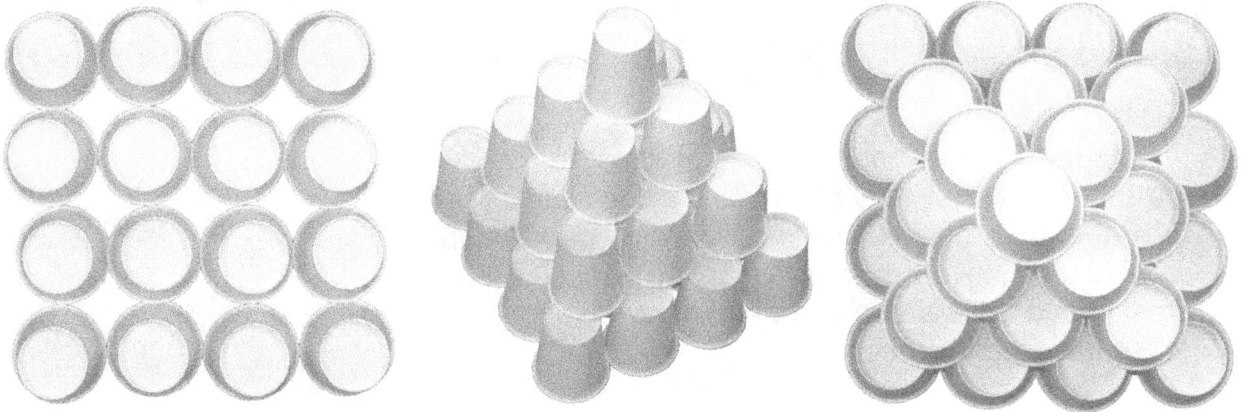

There is another way to build on a rectangular base that is more versatile and more sturdy. The principle involved is the fact that any rectangle can be thought of as a collection of either vertical or horizontal lines. Then, each line can be built upon just like a wall, as illustrated below.

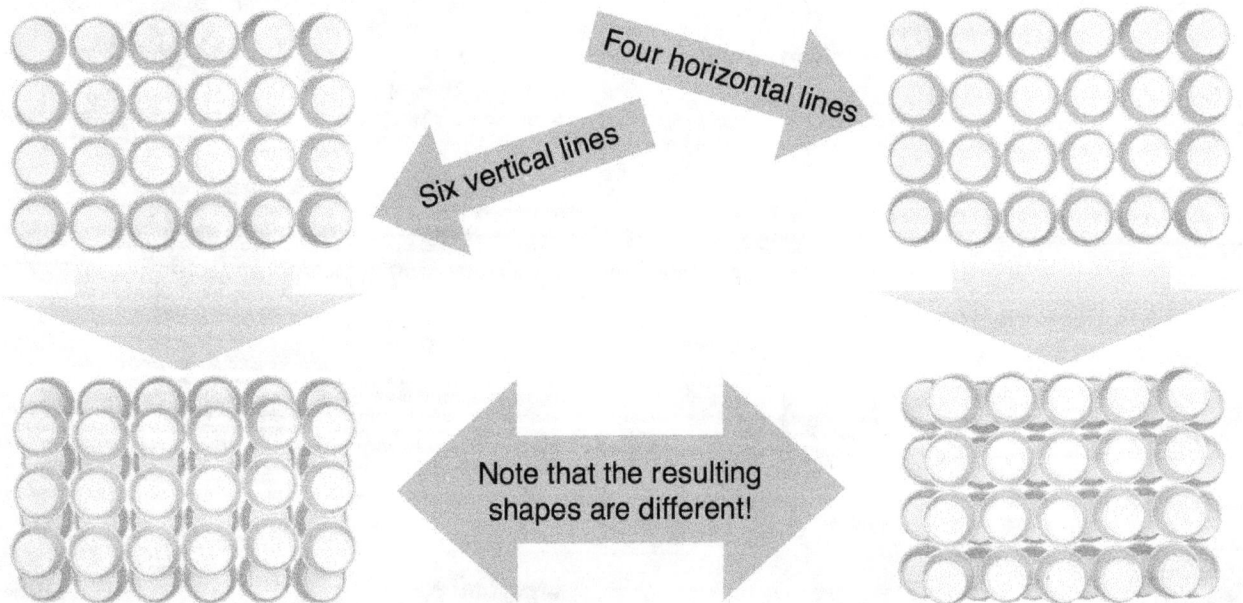

Four horizontal lines

Six vertical lines

Note that the resulting shapes are different!

Here you can see the difference between building a rectangle in vertical or horizontal lines. The tower on the left was made with vertical lines, while the tower on the right was made with horizontal lines. If you wanted, you could continue building upwards on both of these, since they still have a line of cups that can be turned into a wall. If you did this, you would find that the resulting towers would have exactly the same height! In fact, all towers built with this method on a given rectangular base will have the same height.

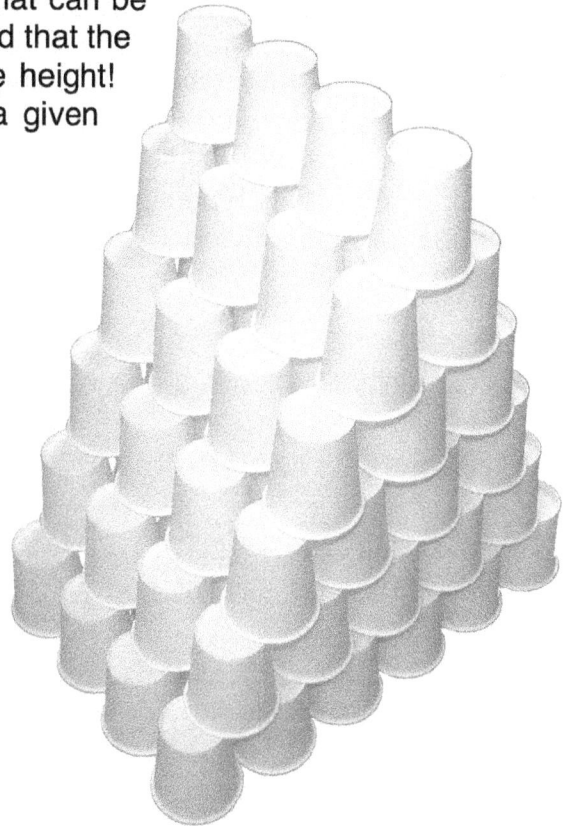

Rectangle towers don't need to be built with only horizontal or only vertical lines. This rectangular tower, for example, was constructed with alternating rows and columns. You can see that all of the even levels decrease in width, while all of the odd levels decrease in length. You could build a rectangle with essentially any combination of horizontal and vertical lines.

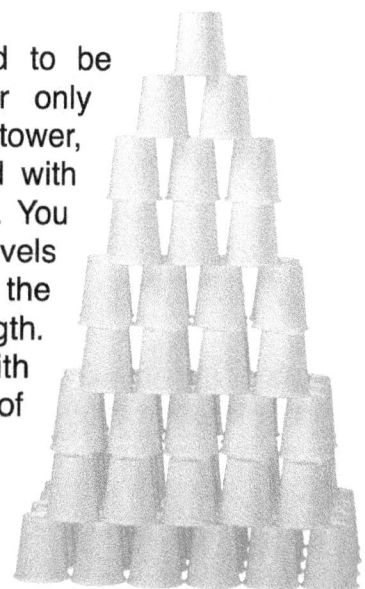

Wall Intersections

One of the unique qualities of walls is that they can intersect with each other. This can be very useful for creating interesting towers. Any wall intersection has the basic form of three lines meeting in a point. The resulting structure has some interesting properties. For example, the center of the tower alternates between being a single cup and a trio of cups, as shown on the right. Each of the walls extending away from the intersection core is called a fin. Intersections are very useful for integrating different types of techniques in one unified paper cup structure.

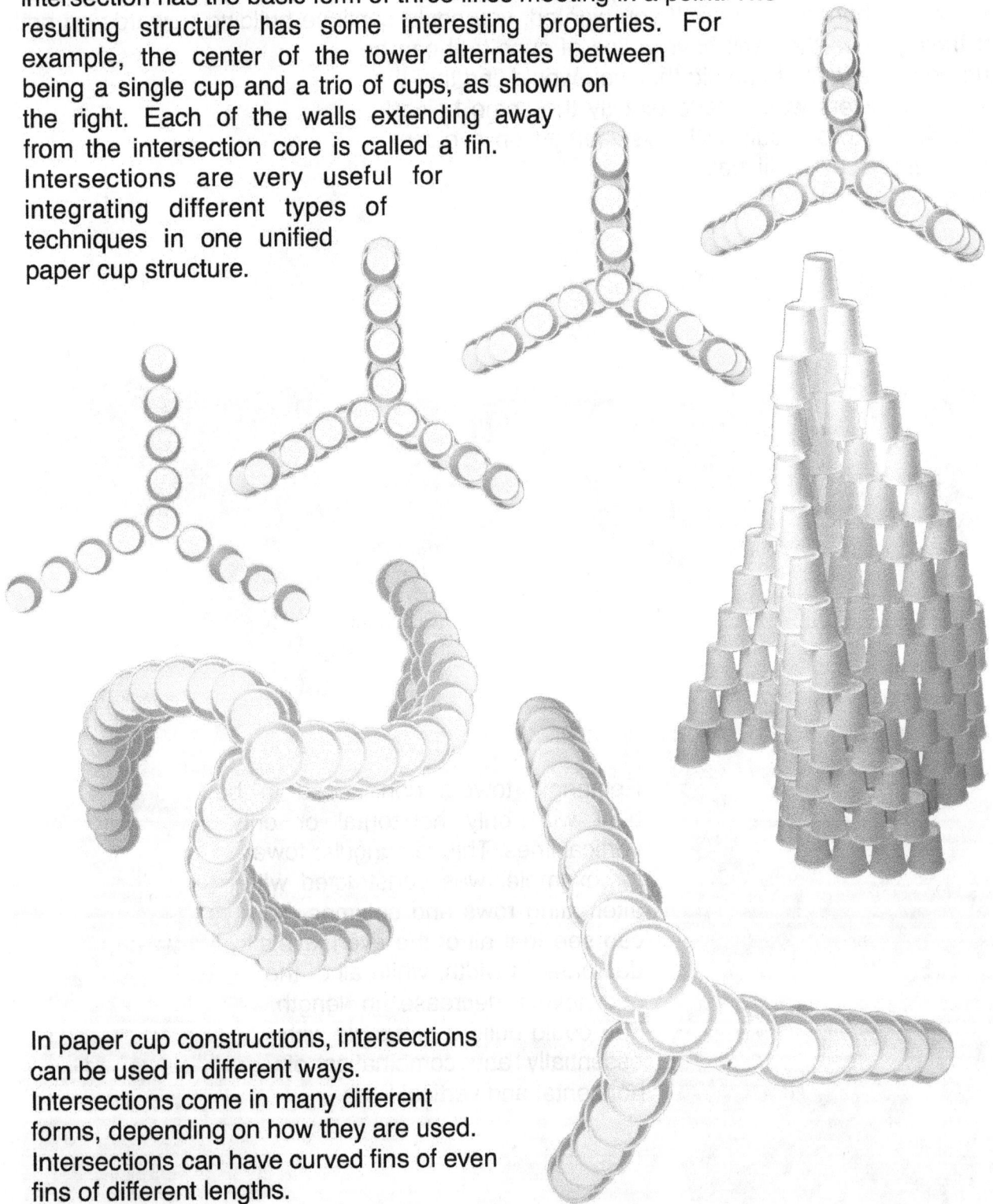

In paper cup constructions, intersections can be used in different ways. Intersections come in many different forms, depending on how they are used. Intersections can have curved fins of even fins of different lengths.

We started this section saying that an intersection is created with three lines intersecting in a point. But if two fins in an intersection are straightened out like a wall, the result is a fin that has been attached to a wall, as in the tower on the left. This principle can be applied to link walls together in many circumstances. A few examples are shown here. See if you can find the intersections in each one!

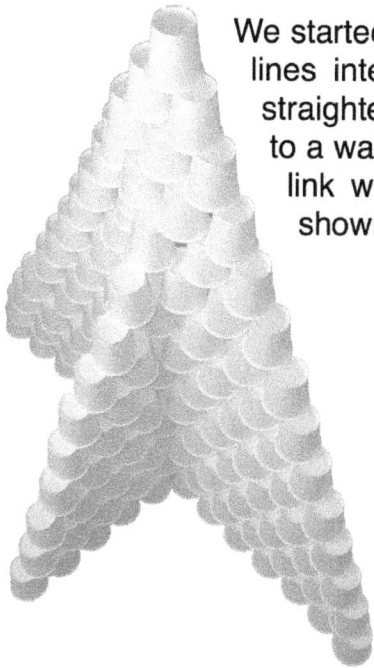

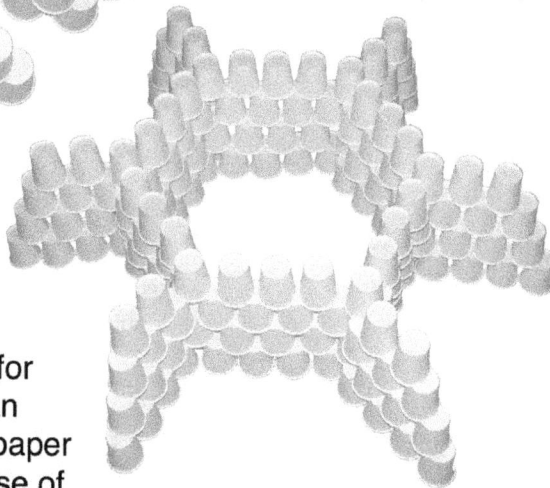

Wall intersections can connect all walls and circles together, resulting in some very interesting possibilities for tower designs. This is an important technique in paper cup construction because of its power to unite otherwise distinct structures.

21

Pyramids

We learned how to make four-sided pyramids in the section on rectangles. In this section, we will discuss triangular pyramids, which are much more versatile.

Obviously, a triangular pyramid begins with a triangle. Each level has a shorter side length than the one below by one cup. Interestingly, the face of a pyramid has the same dimensions as a wall of the same side-length. And both of these have the same dimensions as the pyramid's base.

Pyramids, unlike walls, are built by placing cups on top of groups of three. The tessellation of cups in a pyramid's base are organized in a hexagonal lattice. Interestingly, in the same way that rectangles can be thought of as sets of horizontal or vertical lines, groups of three cups in this hexagonal lattice can be of two different types: those pointing upwards, and those pointing downwards, as shown below.

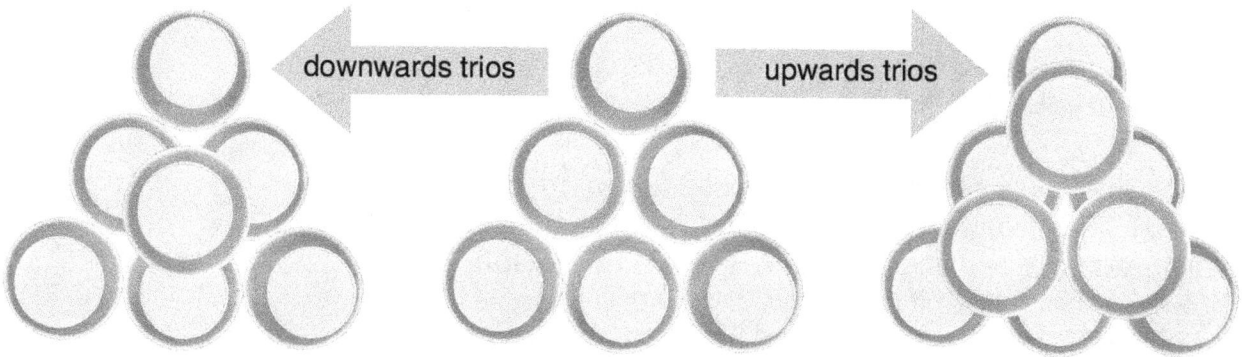

downwards trios

upwards trios

When you place cups on a triangular base, you can either place them on trios of cups pointing in the same direction as the triangular base or the opposite direction as the triangular base. Thus, there are essentially two types of triangular pyramids: normal pyramids and inverse pyramids. Since every level of an inverse pyramid leaves the cups on the corners uncovered, it becomes narrower much faster than a normal pyramid does. This is why an inverse pyramid will be shorter than a normal pyramid of the same base length.

Inverse Pyramid

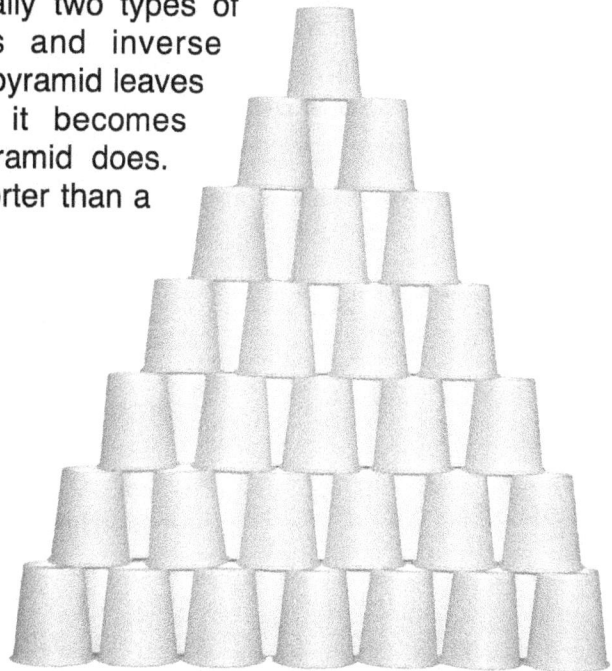

Normal Pyramid

It is clear that the inverse pyramid has a very different structure than the normal pyramid does. One critically important difference is in the organization of the cups in the pyramids' faces. You can see that the inverse pyramid has cups in a linear pattern, while the normal pyramid has cups in an alternating pattern. This difference will be critical when multiple techniques are combined, as we will see in a later section. Another important quality of the inverse pyramid is that buried inside itself is a normal pyramid pointing in the opposite direction. See if you can find it!

Hexagons

In the previous section, we discussed how to build normal and inverse pyramids, each time beginning our tower with a triangular base. There's no reason, however, for us to limit ourselves to only one shape of base. Using the same hexagonal lattice, we can create a wide range of shapes for a tower's base. One particularly interesting shape to build for our base is the hexagon. The reason that this shape is so interesting is that it has no "preferred" direction. In other words, unlike a triangle, it doesn't point in a particular direction. Placing cups on upwards trios would have the same effect as putting cups on downwards trios. Interestingly, if you place cups on upwards trios, the resulting hexagonal shape will still be hexagonal, only a bit squashed. If you continue putting cups only on upwards trios, the subsequent shapes will converge on a downwards pointing triangle, as you can see on the left. At this point, to avoid creating an inverse pyramid, it is necessary to change the direction of the trios. Naturally, the opposite would be true if you were to only place cups on downwards pointing trios; then the subsequent levels converge on an upwards pointing triangle, as on the right.

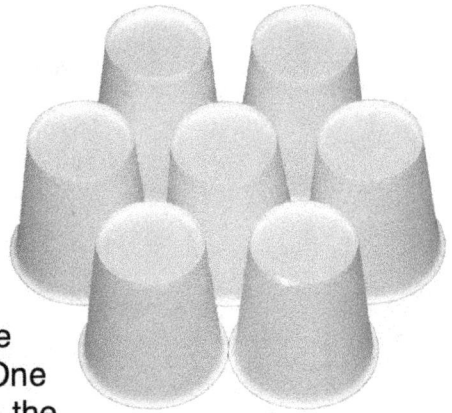

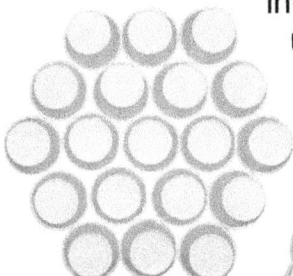

Upwards Trios

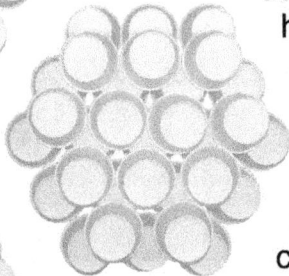

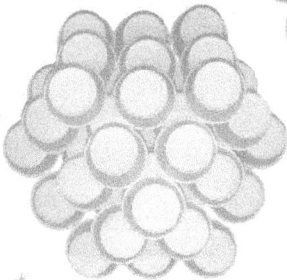

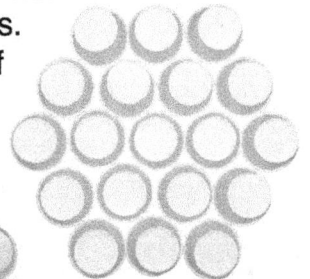

Downwards Trios

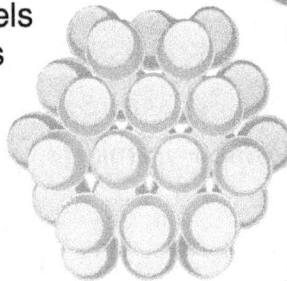

Are these two resulting towers the same or different? Look closely...

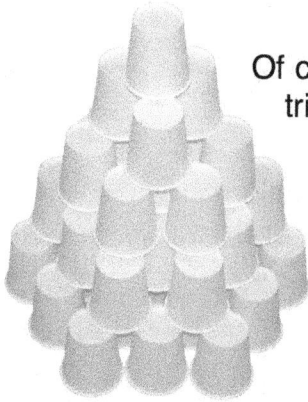

Of course, you could also alternate upwards and downwards pointing trios, like in the hexagon on the left. For that matter you could use essentially any combination of upwards and downwards trios. In fact, so far, the only hexagons that we have analyzed have been regular hexagons, but hexagons can take any proportions. There are endless varieties of interesting shapes that can be made out of a hexagonal lattice of cups. Just think of all the possibilities! A few ideas are shown here.

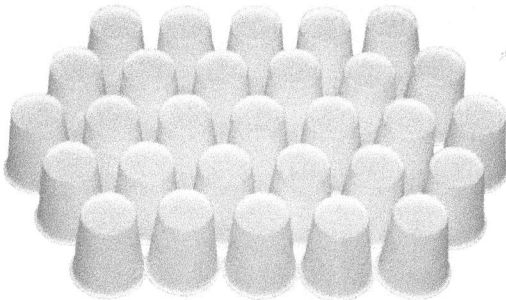

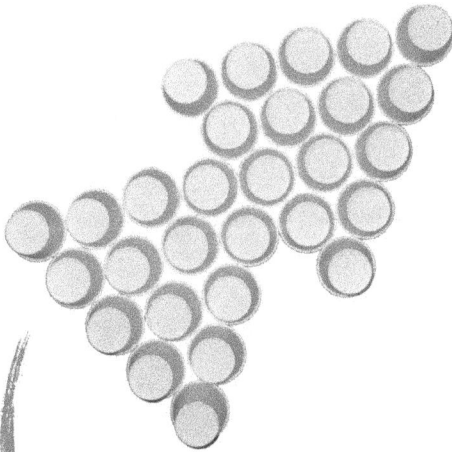

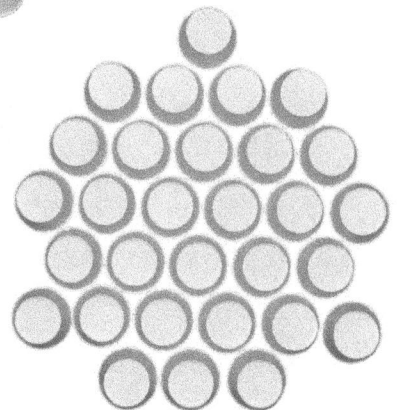

There are some striking similarities between hexagonal bases and rectangular bases. In both cases, we had two options for each level (vertical or horizontal lines; upwards or downwards trios). Furthermore, building a rectangle as vertical lines squashed the shape in the vertical direction and building a hexagon as upwards triangles squashed the shape in the "upwards" direction.

Technique Integrations

Thus far, we've seen two main types of cup construction techniques. On one hand, there are walls and rectangles where each cup is placed on top of two below it, and on the other hand, there are pyramids and hexagons where each cup is placed on a trio below it. In fact, you can include both of these types of techniques in a single structure. Here are some examples of technique integrations.

As in the tower on the right, you can build a triangle with a line of cups at each corner. The result is much like the wall intersections discussed in a previous section, but with a pyramid buried within its core. If you prefer, you could curve the fins on this tower stylistically.

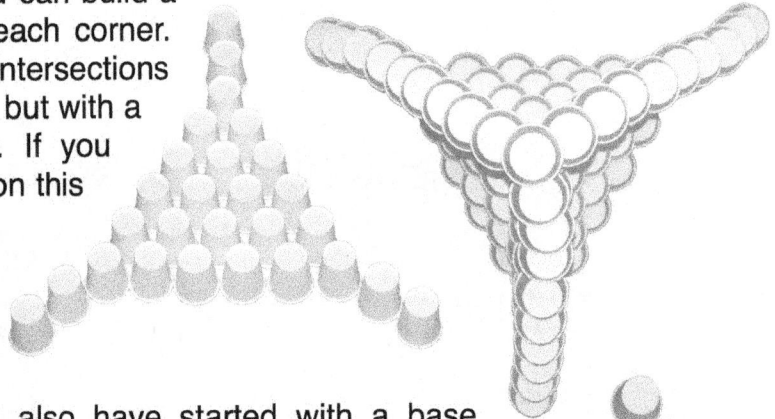

You could also have started with a base made of a rectangle and an adjacent triangle, like the one you see on the right. If you build the triangle as a pyramid and the rectangle in vertical lines, then the resulting integrated structure will look like the tower on the left. Of course, it's important to realize that if the rectangle were built in horizontal lines, the result would have been drastically different because the techniques would not have been able to integrate.

Utilizing multiple techniques dramatically expands the domain of possibilities. A smooth integration between building methods can facilitate a structure that is far greater than the sum of its components. The ability to unite multiple techniques is arguably what crosses the divide between competent construction and insightful artistic expression.

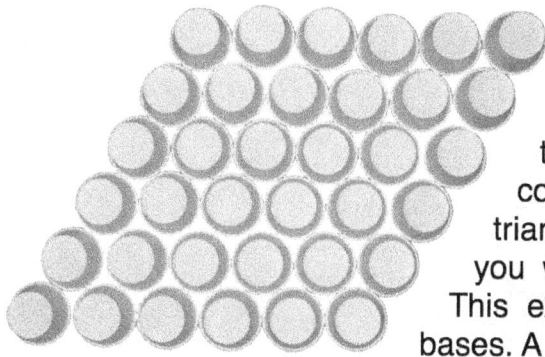

If you start with a line of cups as your base, the only type of tower you can build is a wall. Of course, you could decide how far up the wall to build, but ultimately there would be only one constructive "path" to take. If you begin with a triangular base, however, you can decide whether you wish to build on upwards or downwards trios. This extra level of freedom is a trait of most tower bases. A perfect example of this is the diamond.

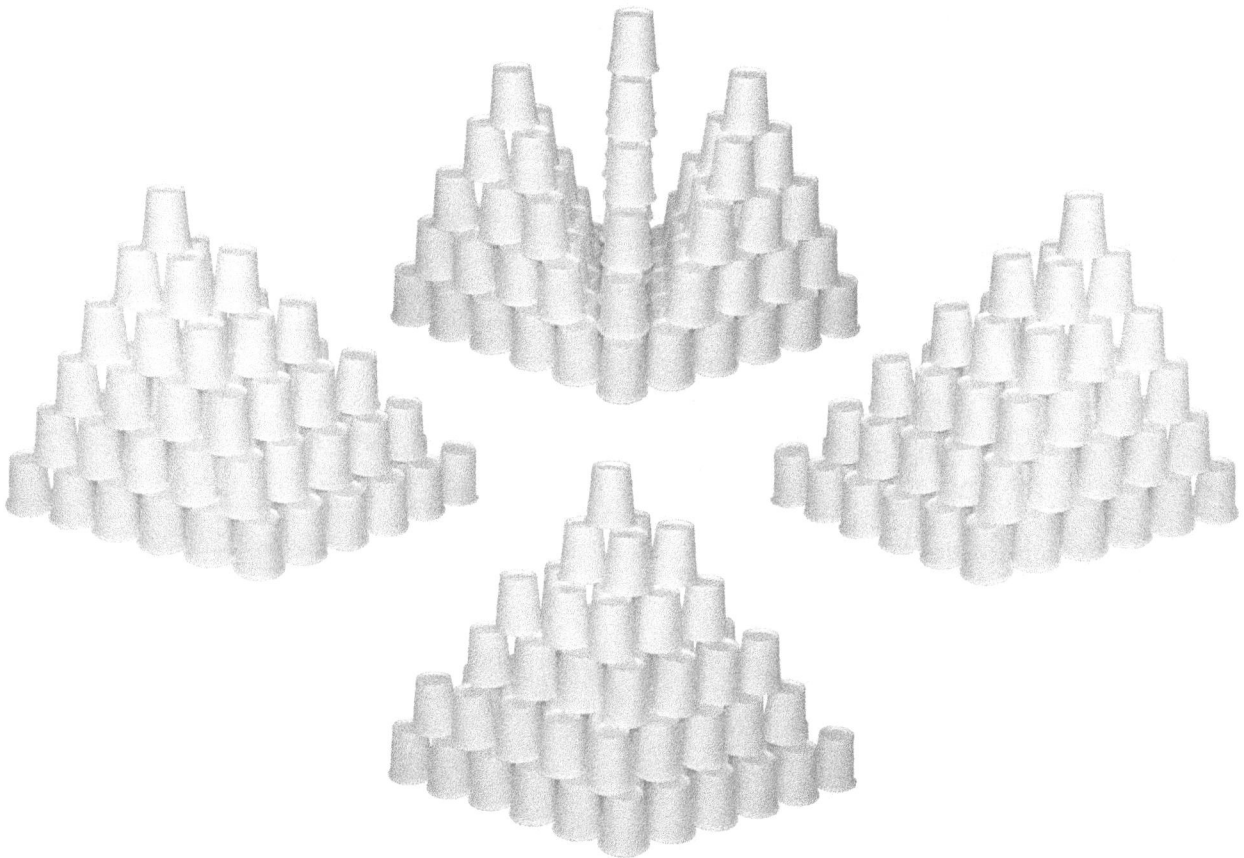

There are many different ways to build on a diamond base, as shown in the towers above. You could build only upwards trios, only downwards trios, or some alternating pattern of upwards and downwards trios. You could even make use of technique integration to build two normal pyramids and a basic wall in the middle resulting in a perfectly symmetric tower like the tower shown on top. How many other ways can you build on a diamond base?

Pillars

On these two pages, we will examine two rather untraditional techniques: pillars and floors. These techniques transcend the conventional tenets of cup construction. There are many more such "non-classical" techniques to be explored. When it comes to paper cups, there are essentially infinite possibilities. You are encouraged to experiment with different structural solutions to find more creative applications of paper cups.

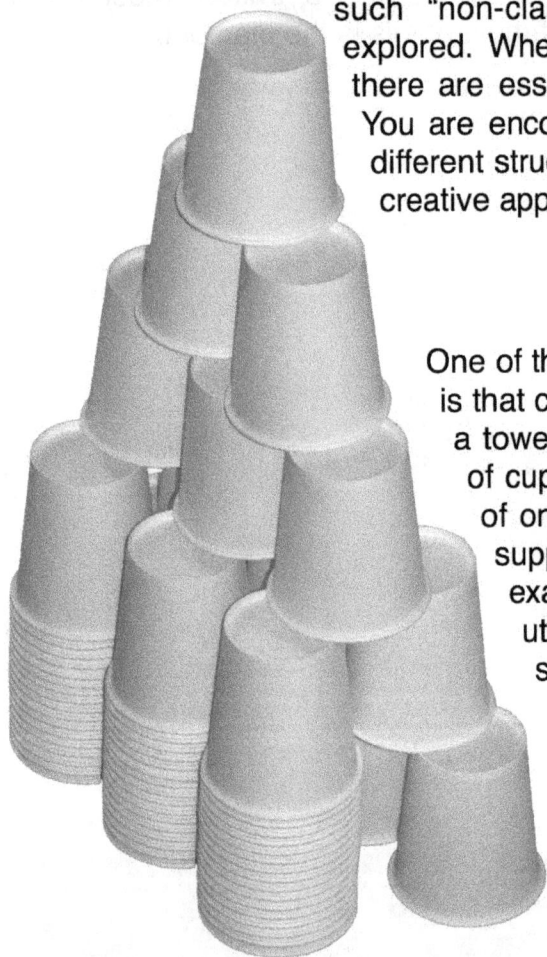

One of the conventional tenets of paper cup construction is that cups should not be stacked inside one another in a tower. Defying this assumption, we find that a stack of cups with a height that is a multiple of one cup's height can be used to support towers in new ways. For example, the tower on the left utilizes pillars as a lateral support structure.

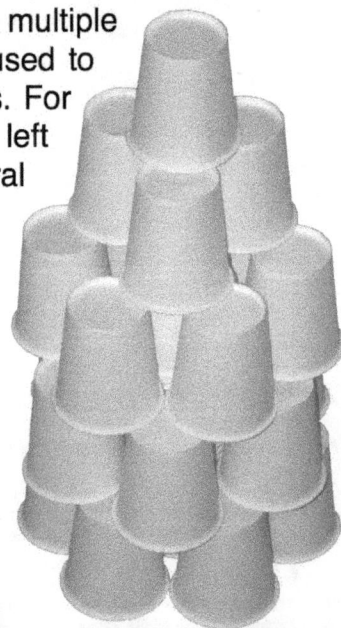

central pillar

Another of many possible uses for pillars in a paper cup tower is shown on the right. A circle was built with a single pillar in the center. This construction allowed for the tower to increase in height without tapering until a certain height, at which point it could be finished like a regular hexagon. Although pillars require many paper cups for a given height, they can be a very versatile building tool.

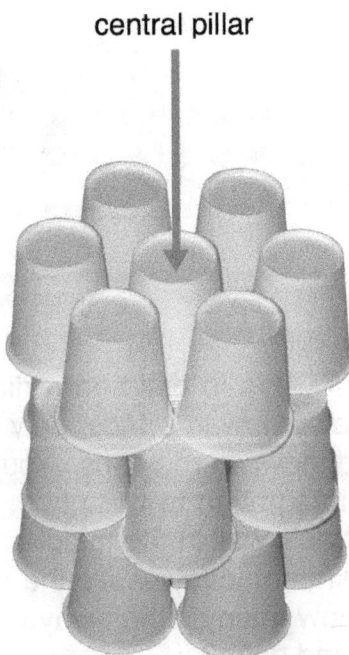

Floors

Another unconventional technique that is worth mentioning is the use of floors. A floor is a flat, rigid, lightweight surface that is used in a paper cup tower. An example of a floor is shown on the right. In this case, it is a round surface that has been placed on top of a circle tower. Even though this technique requires material other than paper cups, it is very powerful because it allows for a tower's fundamental structure to be entirely redefined at given intervals. Here you can see that an initially circular tower was redefined by placing a hexagonal tower on top of the floor. The resulting tower combined both the unrestricted height of a circle tower and the clean termination of a hexagonal tower. Floors can free us from many of the inherent restrictions of paper cup construction, especially that of arches. Usually, paper cups are unable to create arches, domes, and vaults, since they cannot easily be placed on angles or used as keystones. Thus, architectural features such as doors and windows are impossible to construct with paper cups alone. Floors can be used to eliminate this limitation, as in the tower on the right and the wall at the bottom left.

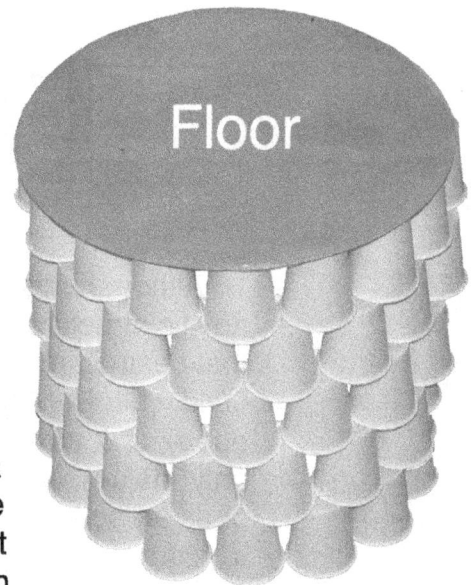

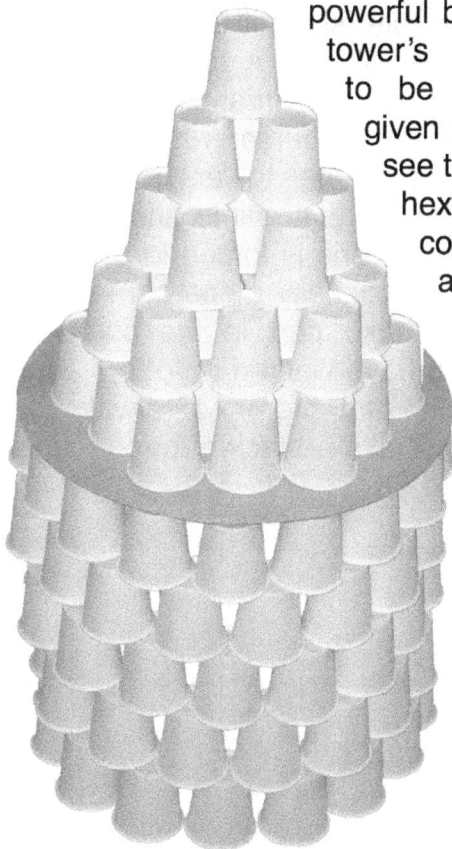

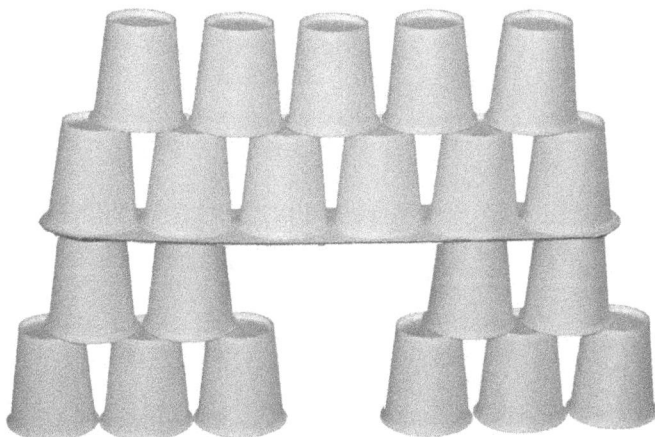

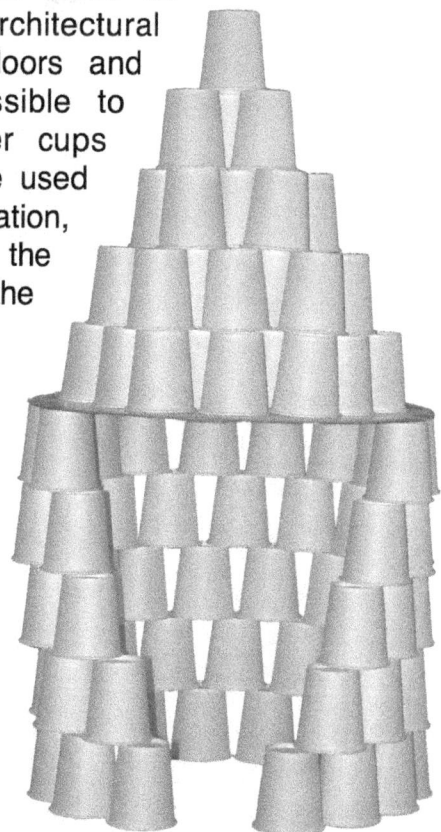

Destruction

Although this book is primarily about the construction and design of artistic structures with paper cups, it's impossible to get around the fact that destructing a tower after it has been built is at least as enjoyable as building it. Unfortunately, towers can "self-destruct" if they are designed poorly or if adverse environmental factors influence them. This fragility only makes tower destruction more enjoyable, since it can be thought of as an act of ownership of the tower's ultimate fate. A good practice is to snap a picture of the finished product before decimating it so that it will live on in memory for all of posterity. Of course, when multiple people are cooperating in building the same tower, a general consensus should be reached about the exact time and method for tower destruction, so that no one is forced to part with the tower before they are emotionally prepared. Indeed, it can be very moving to take part in the complete demolition of something you have worked hard to create. We must remember, though, that there will always be another paper cup tower if you have a stack of paper cups, a creative mind, and a steady hand.

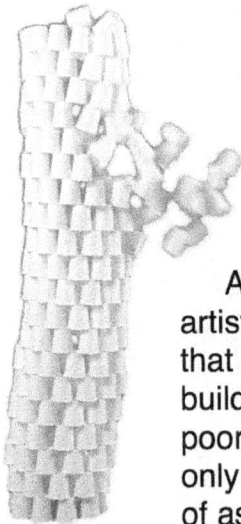

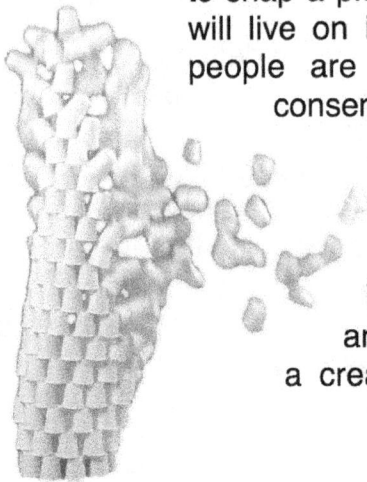

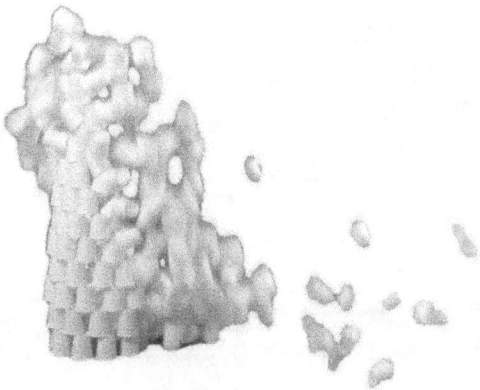

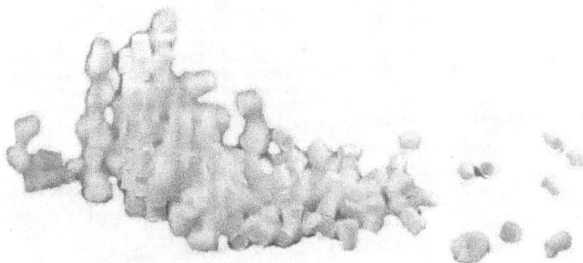

Gallery

The techniques described in this book only scratch the
surface of all the possibilities when it comes to building
with paper cups. This gallery is intended to provide just
a small sample of some of the interesting towers that
can be created with paper cups. Let these two pages
provide inspiration for more of your own paper cup
constructions!

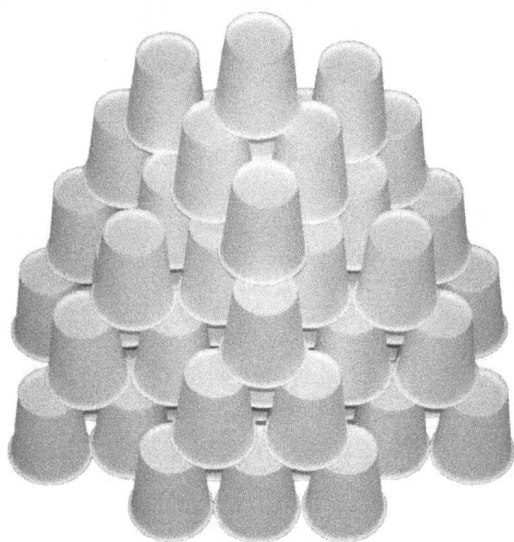

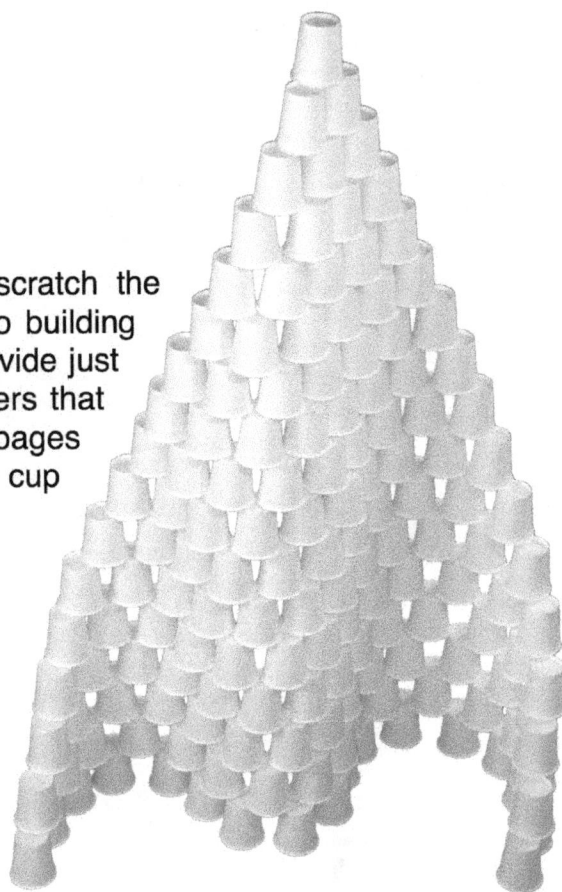

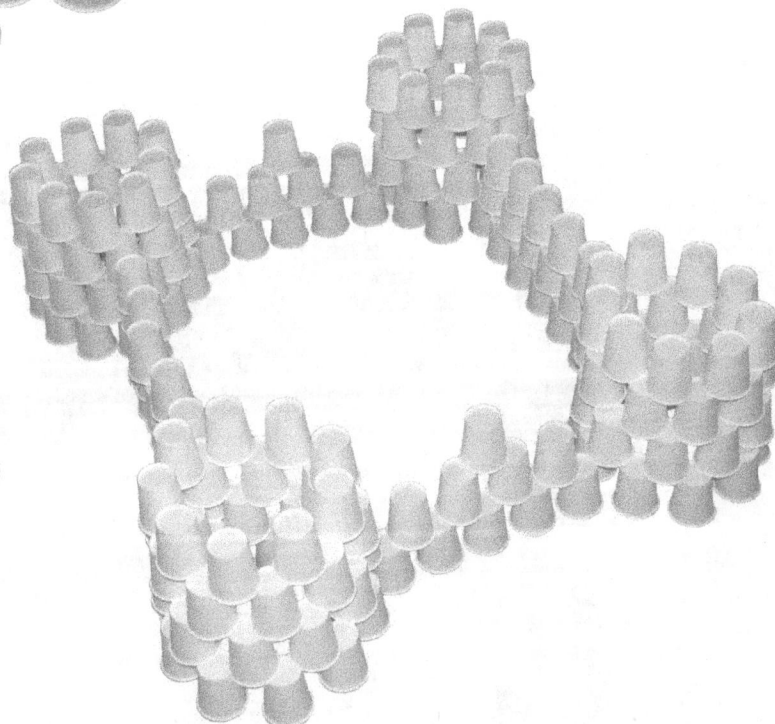

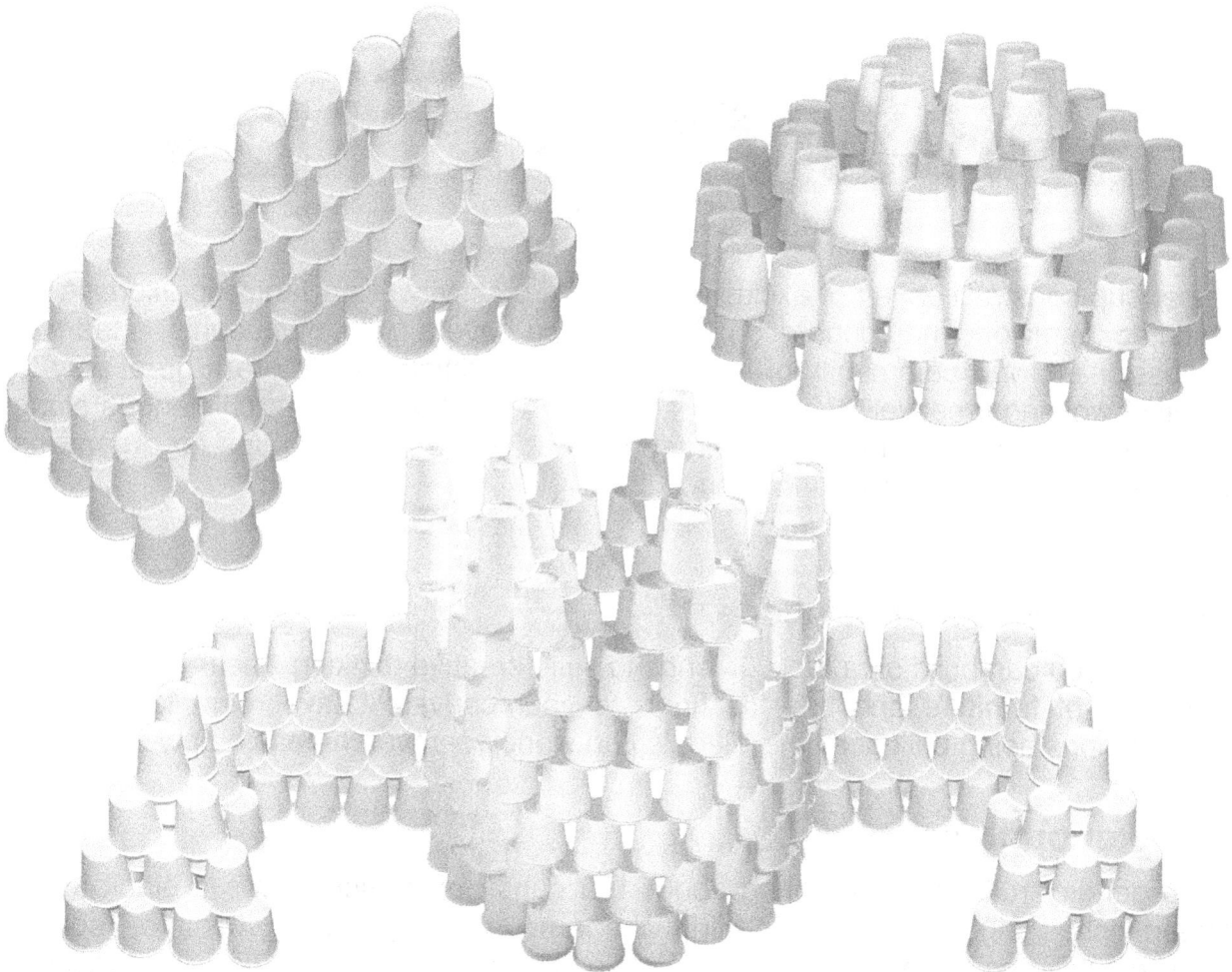

In this book we've explored the fundamentals of paper cup construction, but why stop just with the techniques described here? Try experimenting with glue or tape to hold cups in place. See what happens if you use different sized cups or place them upside down instead. Experiment with different colors and styles if you want to add patterns to your towers. Make multiple towers to create an entire paper cup metropolis. Incorporate other common items into your collection of materials. Can you build with paper plates? Can you use string to hang or support structures? Maybe you can build something other than towers; what about a vehicle or an instrument? Most importantly, always continue to look for surprising new uses for other everyday objects. With creativity and an open mind, an otherwise very ordinary world can become filled with opportunities!

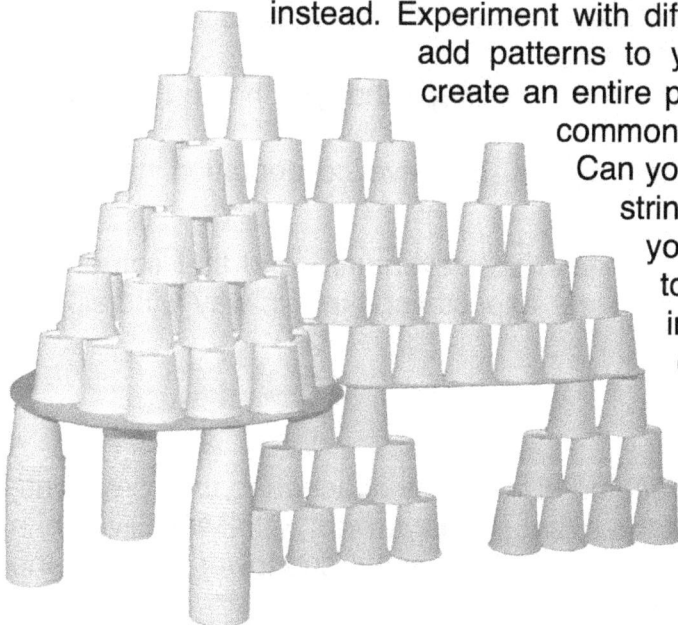

Activity Tips

Paper cup construction is not exclusively a solitary activity. It's a fantastic exercise for fostering teamwork and cooperation. Whether you have a class of students, a team of professionals, or a community of friends, cup construction events are a great way to practice working creatively together to achieve a complex goal with challenges along the way. That sounds a lot like real life, doesn't it? Here are some tips for organizing your own paper cup construction event.

Find plenty of indoor space.

Although you can build on a table, it tends to stifle creative thinking. Clear the center of the room of furniture and use the floor as your canvas. Leave room for multiple constructions being built at a time. People can work wherever there is empty space.

Bring enough paper cups.

As a general rule of thumb, bring about 150 cups per person (that's a stack about fifteen inches tall). Experiment and find what amount works in your scenario. Too few cups will stifle the scale of constructions while too many cups may stifle collaboration.

Set clear expectations.

At the beginning, the protocol for the event should be clear to everyone. For example:

- Be careful around other people's cup constructions. Move cautiously so you don't accidentally create a breeze or knock into something.
- Don't hoard large stacks of cups. Build with the cups that you have. If you want more cups, then collaborate with others.
- Ask people before helping build their towers. Effective collaboration has to be mutually appreciated.

Also remind participants that towers will all fall down eventually and that some may topple during the building process. Setting clear expectations in this way will help the event to run smoothly.

Take photos.

Since people (especially children) can become emotionally attached to their creations, it is advisable to take photos throughout the event so that towers will always live on in memory. Besides, no one will believe the story about the paper cup tower as tall as the ceiling unless you show them the picture!

Circulate the cups.

Begin with paper cups in small stacks distributed around the room. When a tower has been up for a while and has had its picture taken, it should be knocked down so that those cups can be used for other structures. Celebrate the construction, enjoy the destruction, and then start building again. By continuously circulating the cups among the multiple building projects, the environment stays fresh and creative.

Have a plan.

Most people young and old are able to immediately grasp the goal of paper cup construction and need little encouragement to give it a try. However, there may be some who need to be helped into the building process. Have some ideas for possible structures as a catalyst for engagement. Here are some popular structures:

- Circle towers are great for cooperative building and can become very tall.
- Pyramids have a simple mathematical appeal and are very stable.
- Castles with turrets can be built large enough to stand inside of.

Having photos of paper cup constructions available can also help people start generating ideas.

Bring craft supplies.

If you bring other craft supplies like markers, tape, string, cardboard, and paper tubes, it will encourage creative use of the cups that you may have never imagined. Maybe the cups will become decorated as characters or objects. Maybe you can make a draw-bridge with some string and cardboard. Maybe paper tubes and cups can be used to make a musical instrument. Let creativity and ingenuity reign!

Give out some cups.

Every participant can be allowed to have a certain number of cups to take home with them that day (perhaps ten or twenty). This encourages them to continue experimenting with paper cups and may be the start of their own collection of paper cups at home!

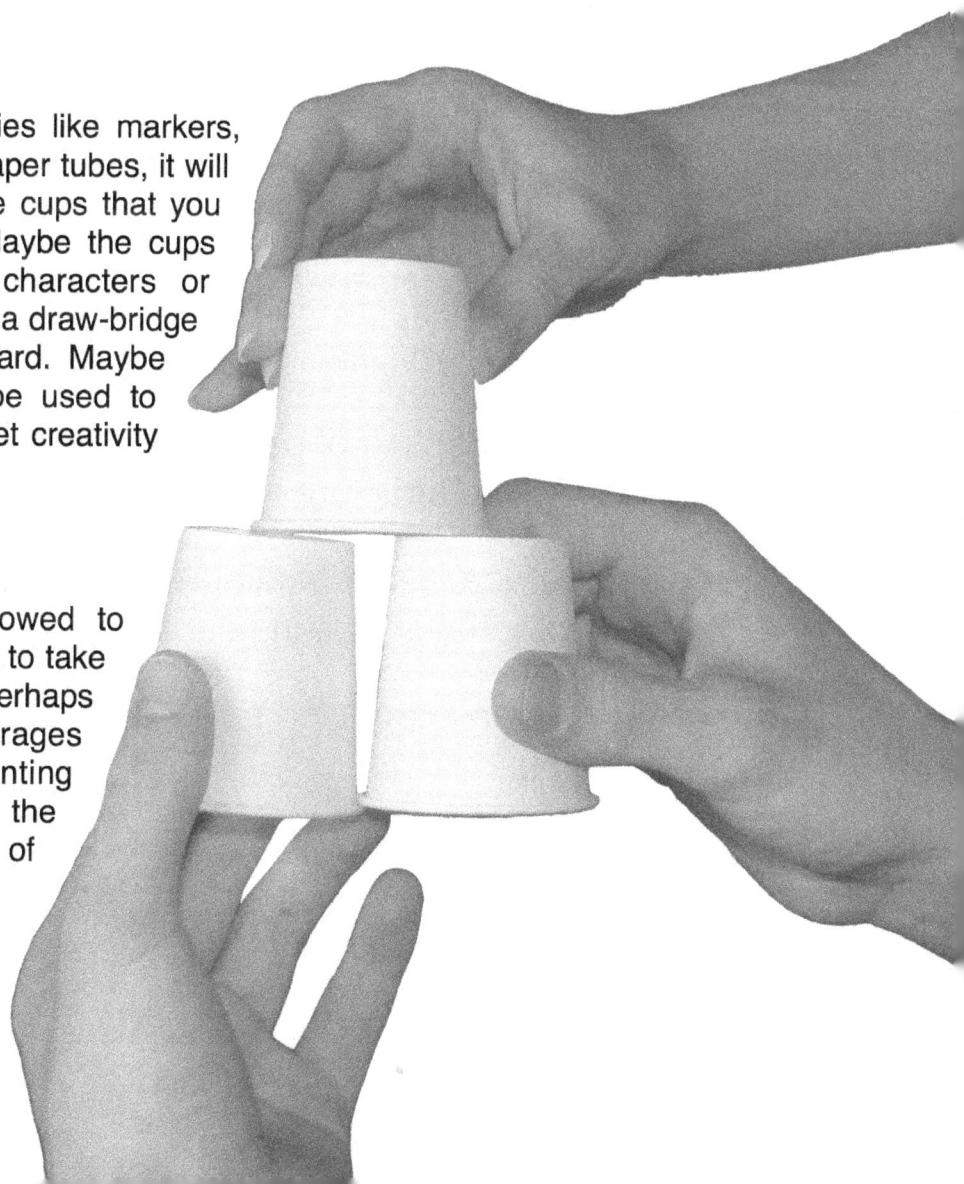

Glossary

base — the lowest level of a tower

circle — any structure built as a "wall" connected to itself at each end, not necessarily with constant curvature, or the base of such a structure

circle termination — a method used to terminate a circle, for example penne or flat terminations

construction — see paper cup construction

cup — see paper cup

fin — a wall extending away from the intersection core in an intersection

floor — a flat, rigid, lightweight surface used as part of a paper cup structure

hexagon — a collection of paper cups arranged in a six-sided convex shape or a structure built on such a base

hexagonal lattice — a repeating arrangement of paper cups, for example hexagonal or rectangular lattice

integration — an integration between two or more techniques or building styles

intersection — an intersection of three walls

intersection core — the central core of an intersection, alternating singles and trios of cups

level — a horizontal cross-section of a tower consisting of all constituent cups at a certain altitude

line — a collection of cups arranged sequentially, not necessarily straight

paper cup — the fundamental structural unit of paper cup construction

paper cup construction — the art and science of creating structures out of paper cups

pillar — a stack of paper cups used as part of a paper cup structure

pyramid — a pyramidal structure, usually with a triangular base, but occasionally with a square base

rectangle — a collection of paper cups arranged in a rectangular lattice or a structure built on such a base

stack — a collection of cups placed inside one another for temporary or permanent storage

technique integration — see integration

termination — see circle termination

triangular pyramid — see pyramid

trio — a collection of three paper cups, all touching each other

wall — a paper cup structure with a line base

wall intersection — see intersection

www.ingramcontent.com/pod-product-compliance
Lightning Source LLC
Chambersburg PA
CBHW080939040426
42443CB00015B/3476